Travel Guide Corfu 2024

Explore Corfu 2024 - Experiencing the Allure of a Greek Paradise

Corfu: A Greek Utopia Beckoning You with Sun Kissed Beaches and Majestic Coastlines

Copyright

TABLE OF CONTENT

10.Conclusion

1.Lasting Impressions of Corfu

2. Your next adventure awaits!

CHAPTER ONE

INTRODUCTION

Welcome to the enchanting island of Corfu, a place where nature's grandeur meets Greek cultural heritage. As your journey begins, prepare to be captivated by breathtaking landscapes, vibrant history, rich traditions, and the warmth of the Corfiot people. Nestled in the crystal-clear waters of the Ionian Sea, Corfu beckons travelers from all around the world to indulge in its unique tapestry of sun-drenched beaches and untamed natural beauty.

Upon your arrival, you'll be greeted by the irresistible aroma of olive trees and the melodic harmonies of traditional Greek music, setting the perfect tone for a memorable vacation. Relax under clear blue skies, immerse yourself in fascinating history, and surrender to the lulling cadence of Corfu's magnetic allure – a journey you will savor for years to come.

Embark on a captivating odyssey as we delve into the charm of Corfu—an island steeped in a resplendent past and brimming with cultural treasures. Since ancient times, this jewel of the Ionian Sea has been coveted for its strategic significance and allure. Traces of its past, left by Byzantines, Venetians, French, and British, still linger amidst its winding lanes, beckoning history enthusiasts seeking to uncover the layers of its storied past.

Corfu's vibrant culture is a mesmerizing fusion of influences from Europe, the Mediterranean, and the Balkans. These influences are most apparent in its architecture, gastronomy, and celebrations. With colorful facades, terracotta roofs, and cobblestone streets, Corfu Town, the island's capital, exudes a captivating ambiance reminiscent of the Venetian era.

As you stroll through its old town, breathing in the fragrance of flowers and hearing snippets of animated conversation, you'll discover the warmth and hospitality of the Corfiot people, who take great pride in preserving their land's traditions. Open-hearted and eager to share their stories, locals will gladly introduce you to the mythical heroes of Greek mythology, narrate tales of seafaring adventures, and indulge you in the pleasures of authentic, mouth watering delicacies.

Corfu's natural splendor acts as the perfect backdrop to its cultural riches. The island's scenic coastline unveils a beguiling panorama of golden sandy beaches, rugged cliffs, olive groves, and azure waters. Whether you seek tranquil idylls or water sports, Corfu's varied shores cater to every taste.

Allow yourself to be enchanted by the magnetic draw of Corfu—a Greek utopia that will leave an indelible imprint on your heart. Journey through the rich tapestry of its history, immerse yourself in its vibrant culture, and be embraced by the genuine warmth of its people. Corfu awaits your exploration, inviting you to write your own chapter in its storied past.

As you set foot on this picturesque island, you are instantly greeted by an atmosphere of warmth and hospitality. Corfu's vibrant spirit is reflected in every nook and cranny, from its bustling markets to its charming villages. Whether you are a history buff, a nature lover, or simply seeking relaxation, Corfu promises an unforgettable experience that will leave you yearning for more.

Welcome to Corfu

Welcome to Corfu, a breathtaking island gem nestled in the azure waters of the Ionian Sea. As you set foot on this enchanting paradise, prepare to experience a harmonious blend of natural beauty, rich history, vibrant culture, and warm hospitality. Corfu, also known as Kerkyra, offers a kaleidoscope of stunning landscapes, an inviting Mediterranean climate, and a wealth of adventures waiting to be discovered.

As you explore the island, you'll encounter a vibrant local culture that revolves around tradition, music, and warm gatherings. Traditional feasts, known as "panigyria," are celebrated with fervor and offer an opportunity to taste authentic Greek delicacies while immersing yourself in lively dances and music. The Corfiot people are known for their strong sense of community and their welcoming nature, ensuring that every visitor feels at home in this Mediterranean paradise.

Nature lovers are in for a treat as Corfu boasts breathtaking landscapes that will leave you in awe. The island's coastline is dotted with hidden coves, turquoise waters, and stunning beaches that invite you to dip your toes and soak in the Mediterranean sun. From the picturesque Paleokastritsa with its crystal-clear waters to the exotic sands of Sidari, each beach offers a unique experience and a chance to unwind in nature's lap.

Venturing inland, you'll find yourself amidst a verdant hinterland, where olive groves, vineyards, and citrus orchards paint a vibrant picture of the island's natural beauty. Take a leisurely stroll through charming villages like Old Perithia or explore the rugged countryside on one of the many hiking trails, allowing you to uncover the hidden gems and breathtaking vistas that make Corfu truly extraordinary.

Whether you choose to delve into the island's rich history, indulge in its vibrant culture, or simply relax on its sun-kissed shores, Corfu promises an experience like no other. So come, immerse yourself in the magic of this Greek paradise, and let Corfu captivate your heart and soul with its timeless charm.

The Charm of Corfu: An Overview of its History, Culture, and People

History

To truly understand the allure of Corfu, one must delve into its captivating history, explore its rich culture, and embrace the warmth of its people. Over the centuries, this island has been shaped by a tapestry of civilizations, each leaving its own indelible mark.

Corfu's history dates back to ancient times, with legends linking it to the Greek hero Odysseus. Throughout the years, the island has been influenced by Greek, Roman, Venetian, French, and British cultures, resulting in a unique blend that is distinctly Corfiot. From the imposing forts built by the Venetians to the elegant palaces adorned with French-inspired architecture, Corfu's historical landmarks take you on a captivating journey through time.

Immerse yourself in the captivating past of Corfu, where tales of ancient civilizations intertwine with stories of medieval conquests and Venetian influence. Steeped in a glorious history, this island has borne witness to the events that have shaped Greece and Europe. From the Mycenaean era to Roman occupation, Byzantine rule to

Venetian dominion, Corfu's past reveals itself at every turn.

Culture

Corfu's cultural tapestry is a diverse fusion of influences from its conquerors and inhabitants throughout the centuries. Greek customs, Venetian traditions, and British legacies, all meld together to create a vibrant and unique culture. Delve into the island's rich art scene, where theaters, galleries, and museums showcase the talent and creativity of local artists. Experience authentic Greek cuisine, with its tantalizing flavors and tantalizing aromas that will leave your taste buds longing for more.

People

No exploration of Corfu is complete without encountering its warm and welcoming people. Known for their friendliness and hospitality, the Corfiots will embrace you with open arms, eager to share their love for their island paradise. Engage in conversations with the locals, learn about their customs and traditions, and discover the hidden corners of Corfu that only insiders know. Let their stories and anecdotes bring the island to life, giving you a deeper understanding of its culture and heritage.

Corfu beckons you with its sunkissed beaches and majestic coastlines, inviting you into a world where time seems to stand still. The sun-drenched shores offer a haven for relaxation and leisure, with crystal-clear waters lapping at your feet. Dip your toes in the azure sea, indulge in sunbathing, or partake in thrilling water sports that will invigorate your senses.

Beyond the beaches, the island's landscape presents a captivating mosaic of olive groves, lush vineyards, and cypress-clad hills. Take a stroll through the narrow streets of the Old Town, a UNESCO World Heritage site, and marvel at its Venetian architecture and charming alleyways. Lose yourself in the labyrinthine lanes, where every corner unveils a hidden treasure.

Venture further inland, and you'll encounter picturesque villages nestled in verdant valleys, where time-honored traditions thrive. From the traditional village of Paleokastritsa, known for its stunning coastal vistas, to the mountainous retreat of Pelekas, adorned with panoramic views from its hilltop perch, Corfu offers a plethora of experiences for every traveler.

Uncover the island's rich history by exploring its ancient sites and architectural wonders. The Achilleion Palace, a testament to Empress Elisabeth of Austria's love affair with the island, exudes opulence and grandeur. Wander through the ruins of the Temple of Artemis, an archaeological treasure steeped in myth and legend. Let each step transport you back in time, revealing the stories of the civilizations that once thrived on this majestic island.

As night falls, prepare to be mesmerized by Corfu's vibrant nightlife. Enjoy a leisurely dinner at a seaside taverna, savoring sumptuous Greek delicacies while listening to the soft melody of live music. Discover the bustling bars and clubs, where you can dance the night away in true Greek style.

Corfu, the Greek paradise beckoning you, awaits your arrival. Let its awe-inspiring beauty and rich history captivate your soul and create memories that will last a lifetime. Come and explore the undiscovered corners of this island gem, embracing the warmth of its people and experiencing the true essence of Corfu.

CHAPTER TWO

PLANNING YOUR TRIP

When to Visit Corfu:

Corfu is a stunning destination that offers a variety of experiences throughout the year. However, the best time to visit Corfu is during the spring (April-May) and fall (September-October) seasons. During these months, you can avoid the crowds and enjoy pleasant weather with temperatures ranging from 20 to 30 degrees Celsius (68 to 86 degrees Fahrenheit). The island is bathed in blooming flowers during spring, creating a picturesque delight for nature enthusiasts. Alternatively, in the fall, the island's verdant landscape transforms into a tapestry of warm, autumnal hues.

How to Get to Corfu:

Getting to Corfu is made easy by various transportation options. The most common way to reach this enchanting island is by air. Ioannis Kapodistrias International Airport serves as the main gateway for international and domestic flights. Multiple airlines operate direct flights to Corfu from major cities across Europe, making it accessible for travelers from all corners of the world.

For those traveling by sea, there are ferry connections available from the Greek mainland and other nearby islands. Ferries offer a scenic and leisurely journey, allowing you to soak in the beauty of the surrounding Ionian Sea.

Where to Stay in Corfu:

Corfu boasts a wide range of accommodation options to meet diverse preferences and budgets. Whether you seek luxurious resorts, boutique hotels, secluded villas, traditional guesthouses, or budget-friendly hostels, Corfu has it all.

In Corfu Town, the island's captivating capital, you can find hotels brimming with history, elegant architecture, and modern amenities. Staying in the heart of the town allows you to immerse yourself in its vibrant atmosphere, exploring its narrow streets, historic sites, and charming cafes.

If you prefer a quieter setting, consider the northern part of the island, which offers serene coastal resorts nestled amidst olive groves. These areas provide easy access to the island's sandy beaches and picturesque villages, allowing for a peaceful and rejuvenating getaway.

For a more lively experience, the southern part of the island presents vibrant beach resorts such as Kavos, known for its energetic nightlife and bustling beachside bars.

Essential Travel Information:

Research and Plan: Start by researching the island's popular attractions, cultural customs, and local transportation options. This will help you make the most of your time in Corfu. Plan your itinerary accordingly.

Pack Light: Corfu has a pleasant Mediterranean climate, so it's advisable to pack light and breathable clothing. Don't forget sunscreen, sunglasses, and a hat to protect yourself from the sun. Don't forget to bring a swimsuit, as Corfu's mesmerizing beaches will tempt you to take a refreshing dip in the turquoise waters

Currency: The currency in Corfu is the Euro. ATMs can be found throughout the island, and credit cards are widely accepted in most establishments. Ensure you have some cash on hand.

Language: Greek is the primary language spoken in Corfu. However, English is widely spoken in tourist areas, making communication easier for international travelers. Familiarize yourself with basic Greek phrases and greetings to connect with the friendly locals. Understanding simple social norms, such as the concept of "filoxenia" (hospitality), will enhance your experience and leave a positive impression on the islanders.

Health and Safety: Corfu maintains a high standard of healthcare facilities. It is advisable to have travel insurance to cover any medical emergencies. Additionally, be vigilant of your surroundings and belongings to ensure a safe and enjoyable stay. It's also wise to carry a first aid kit and any necessary medications you may need during your trip.

Local Customs: Embrace the local customs and traditions of Corfu by respecting the cultural norms and etiquette. Modest clothing may be required while visiting religious sites, and it is polite to greet locals with a warm smile and a simple "Yasou" (hello) or "Efharisto" (thank you).

Transportation: Corfu has a well-connected public transportation system, including buses, taxis, and rental cars. Familiarize yourself with the routes and schedules to navigate the island conveniently. Public transportation options in Corfu include buses and taxis, which provide convenient ways to explore the island. Rental cars and scooters are also available if you prefer independent transportation.

Explore Corfu Town: Start your trip by visiting Corfu Town, the island's charming capital. Get lost in the narrow streets of the Old Town, visit historic landmarks like the

Old Fortress, and immerse yourself in the local culture and architecture.

Beach Hopping: Corfu boasts some of the most stunning beaches in Greece. Don't limit yourself to just one beach – rent a car or a scooter to explore the coastline. From the famous Paleokastritsa to the quieter Agios Georgios, be sure to visit a variety of beaches that suit your preferences.

Taste Local Cuisine: Greek cuisine is renowned worldwide, and Corfu's unique dishes won't disappointed. Be sure to explore the local restaurants and try traditional dishes like moussaka and tzatziki. Take advantage of the island's fresh seafood, devour some delicious souvlaki, and don't miss out on trying the local specialty called pastitsada.

Visit the Achilleion Palace: This beautiful palace, once owned by the Empress of Austria, Elisabeth of Bavaria (Sisi), offers breathtaking views and intricate architecture. Marvel at the statues and gardens, and experience the grandeur of this historical gem.

Explore the Villages: Corfu is home to picturesque villages that reflect the island's rich history and culture. Visit places like Sidari, Kassiopi, or Pelekas to get a taste of traditional life, interact with locals, and discover hidden gems off the beaten path.

Take a Boat Trip: Discover the hidden coves and secret swimming spots by taking a boat trip around the island. Cruise along the coastline, dive into crystal-clear waters, and enjoy stunning vistas that can only be reached by sea.

Enjoy Outdoor Activities: If you're an outdoor enthusiast, Corfu won't disappoint. Go hiking or take a stroll through the Corfu Trail to see the island's stunning landscapes. You can also try water sports like snorkeling, swimming, boat trips,diving, or windsurfing to make the most of the island's clear waters.

Embrace the Nightlife: Corfu has a buzzing nightlife scene, especially in places like Kavos and Corfu Town. Whether you're looking to party until the early hours or enjoy a laid-back evening at a beachside tavern, take the opportunity to experience the island's vibrant atmosphere after the sun goes down.

Local Etiquette: Greeks are known for warm hospitality, so it's polite to learn a few local customs. For example, it's customary to greet people with a friendly "kalimera" (good morning) and "efharisto" (thank you).

Remember, these are just a few guidelines to make your travel experience in Corfu enjoyable and stress-free. Feel free to personalize your trip and follow your own interests and passions. Corfu awaits your arrival, embracing you with its irresistible beauty and warm Greek hospitality. Enjoy your explorations, and create unforgettable memories on this Greek paradise island!

CHAPTER THREE

EXPLORING THE ISLAND

Corfu Town and Historical Landmarks

Corfu Town, with its rich history and captivating architecture, is a must-visit destination on the island of Corfu. As you stroll through its charming streets, you will be spellbound by the fusion of Venetian, French, and British architectural influences. The historical landmarks narrate the island's journey through time. Here are some key highlights to explore:

1.1 Old Fortress and New Fortress

Standing tall at the eastern entrance of the town, the Old Fortress (Paleo Frourio) offers panoramic views of the town and the Ionian Sea. Its impressive architecture and fortified walls date back to the Byzantine era. The New Fortress (Neo Frourio), on the other hand, adorns the western side of Corfu Town and showcases Venetian military engineering at its finest.

1.2 Liston Promenade and Spianada Square

Embrace the vibrant atmosphere of Liston Promenade, lined with beautiful arches and adorned with cafes and shops. Adjacent to it is the majestic Spianada Square, one of the largest in Europe, where you can enjoy leisurely walks or even catch a cricket match—a quintessentially British pastime.

1.3 Achilleion Palace

Step into the world of myth and ancient Greece at the Achilleion Palace, a neoclassical gem built by Empress Elisabeth of Austria. Admire its stunning gardens, adorned with statues and manicured landscapes. The palace offers breathtaking views of the coast and is a true testament to Corfu's allure.

Coastal Villages and Traditional Culture

Escape to the tranquil coastal villages of Corfu, where time seems to stand still and traditional Greek culture thrives. These enchanting villages welcome you with open arms, offering an authentic experience of Corfiot life.

2.1 Palaiokastritsa

Perched on the rugged western coast, Palaiokastritsa boasts crystal-clear turquoise waters and breathtaking cliffs. Explore its charming monastery, nestled on a hilltop, and dive into its hidden caves to marvel at the underwater beauty.

2.2 Kassiopi

Seated on the northeastern side of the island, Kassiopi is steeped in both history and idyllic charm. Wander through its narrow streets lined with tavernas, boutiques, and ancient ruins. The Byzantine castle overlooks the azure sea and invites you to relish the picturesque vistas.

2.3 Benitses

Located on the southeast coast, Benitses is a traditional fishing village that offers a glimpse into the daily life of Corfiot fishermen. Stroll along the waterfront, indulge in fresh seafood at its tavernas, and soak up the sun on its pebbled beaches.

Natural Wonders of Corfu

Corfu's natural beauty is truly awe-inspiring, captivating visitors with its pristine beaches, lush green landscapes, and magical hidden gems.

3.1 Sidari and Canal d'Amour

Sidari, a northern coastal village, is famous for the stunning Canal d'Amour—a breathtaking natural formation of sandstone cliffs and narrow passageways. Explore these impressive rock formations, said to have mystical powers, and take a dip in the crystal-clear turquoise waters.

3.2 Mount Pantokrator

For adventure-seekers, Mount Pantokrator offers sweeping views of the island from its 906-meter summit. Explore its dense forests, trekking trails, and discover the beautiful Byzantine monastery that rests at its peak.

3.3 Lake Korission

A true haven for nature enthusiasts, Lake Korission is a lagoon-like paradise nestled between golden sand dunes. Home to a diverse range of flora and fauna, it invites you to enjoy peaceful walks, bird-watching, or simply basking in the beauty of its surroundings.

Outdoor Activities and Adventure Sports

Corfu offers an abundance of outdoor pursuits and thrilling activities that cater to adventure-seekers of all kinds. Whether you prefer thrill-seeking adventures or leisurely exploration, the island has something for everyone.

4.1 Water Sports

Embark on exhilarating water sports adventures, from windsurfing and jet-skiing to parasailing and sailing. The sparkling waters, favorable wind conditions, and professional instructors make Corfu the ideal playground for aquatic enthusiasts.

4.2 Hiking and Cycling

Uncover Corfu's picturesque landscapes on foot or by bike, as the island is blessed with numerous trails and paths. Meander through verdant olive groves, explore hidden coves, and breathe in the invigorating scent of cypress trees as you immerse yourself in nature.

4.3 Horseback Riding

Discover the island's hidden beauty on horseback, riding along sandy shores, through rolling hills, and beneath the shade of ancient olive trees. With experienced guides leading the way, you can appreciate the island's landscapes from a different perspective.

Corfu promises an extraordinary journey filled with historic landmarks, coastal villages steeped in tradition, captivating natural wonders, and an array of thrilling outdoor activities. Embrace the allure of this Greek paradise and create memories that will last a lifetime.

CHAPTER FOUR

BEACHES AND COASTLINES

Corfu, a Greek paradise, is blessed with an abundance of pristine beaches that leave travelers spellbound. With its warm Mediterranean climate, Corfu boasts an idyllic coastline that stretches across its beautiful shores. Whether you are seeking a tranquil retreat or an adventurous getaway, the top beaches in Corfu offer something for everyone. Let's embark on a journey to explore the finest beaches this Greek gem has to offer.

Top Beaches in Corfu

Corfu, also known as the Emerald Isle of Greece, is home to some of the most breathtaking beaches in the world. From golden stretches of sand to hidden coves framed by dramatic cliffs, each beach offers a unique and mesmerizing experience. In this chapter, we will dive into the top beaches in Corfu, where you can soak up the sun, indulge in turquoise waters, and create unforgettable memories.

1. Glyfada Beach:

Situated on the west coast, Glyfada Beach boasts powdery white sand and crystal-clear waters that shimmer under the golden sun. Its natural beauty, combined with its crystal-clear waters, ensures a memorable beach experience. Take a leisurely stroll along the soft sand, feel the warmth of the sun, and dive into the sparkling waters for a refreshing swim. If you seek adventure, try your hand at exciting water sports such as parasailing and jet skiing. This Blue Flag awarded beach is perfect for sun worshippers, as it offers various amenities such as beach bars, sunbeds, and water sports facilities. Whether you prefer a lazy day under an umbrella or windsurfing across the waves, Glyfada Beach has you covered.

2. Paleokastritsa Beach:
Nestled on the western side of the island lies Paleokastritsa Beach, a true postcard-worthy paradise. Surrounded by lush green cliffs, this idyllic beach offers visitors a tranquil retreat with its calm turquoise waters. Take a boat tour to explore nearby sea caves or try scuba diving to discover the hidden underwater world teeming with marine life. Paleokastritsa Beach is a must-visit for those seeking serenity and natural beauty.

3. Sidari Beach:
Located on the northern coast of Corfu, Sidari Beach is famous for its unique rock formations known as the "Canal d'Amour" or "Channel of Love." Legend has it that

couples who swim through the narrow channel will be blessed with eternal love. Beyond its romantic allure, Sidari Beach offers golden sands and azure waters ideal for sunbathing and swimming. Explore the charming beachfront town of Sidari, indulge in local cuisine, or simply unwind on this enchanting beach.

4. Agios Gordios Beach:
Situated on the western side of the island, Agios Gordios Beach is a paradise for nature enthusiasts. With a backdrop of verdant cliffs, this long sandy beach offers a soothing atmosphere and stunning panoramic views. Explore the nearby village of Agios Gordios, where you can taste authentic Greek delicacies and immerse yourself in the local culture. Whether you're seeking relaxation or adventure, Agios Gordios Beach is sure to captivate you.

5. Kontogialos Beach:

Nestled majestically on the western coast of Corfu lies Kontogialos Beach, an untouched gem awaiting your discovery. Surrounded by stunning cliffs and dense greenery, this beach enchants visitors with its unspoiled beauty. The golden sand, coupled with the clear blue sea, provides the perfect setting for a day in paradise. Participate in adrenaline-pumping water sports, or simply unwind with a book as gentle sea breezes caress your skin.

6. Kavos Beach:

For those seeking a lively beach experience with party vibes and water sports galore, Kavos Beach is the place to be. Situated in the southern part of Corfu, this energetic beach offers an array of exhilarating activities. Surfing, jet skiing, and banana boat rides are just a few options for thrill-seekers. Dance to vibrant music, sip refreshing cocktails, and indulge in the vibrant nightlife that Kavos has to offer while embracing the true essence of summer fun.

Hidden Gems - Secluded Beaches

While Corfu's famous beaches offer incredible beauty and relaxation, the island also harbors some hidden gems - secluded beaches tucked away from the tourist crowds. For the adventurous souls who prefer ultimate seclusion, Corfu is home to hidden gems - secluded beaches that offer privacy and a sense of tranquility away from the crowds. Brace yourself for a secret rendezvous with solitude, as we unveil Corfu's best-kept secrets. Here are a few serene slices of heaven waiting to be discovered:

1. Myrtiotissa Beach:
Nestled between the cliffs on the west coast, Myrtiotissa Beach is an untouched paradise only accessible through a narrow path. With its pristine beauty and nudist-friendly atmosphere, it is a haven for

those seeking wilderness and solitude. Its jade waters and golden sands make it a true hidden gem.

2. Arkoudilas Beach:
Located on the southern tip of the island, Arkoudilas Beach is a small cove nestled at the foot of imposing cliffs. Reachable only by a scenic hike or by boat, this secluded beach offers seclusion like no other. Sunbathe on the smooth pebbles, indulge in a picnic with panoramic views, and revel in the tranquility of this hidden paradise.

3. Porto Timoni Beach:
Tucked away on the northwestern coast of Corfu, Porto Timoni Beach is a hidden gem accessible only by a challenging hike. The reward at the end of the trek is an awe-inspiring panorama of twin beaches separated by a narrow strip of land. Surrounded by striking cliffs and azure waters, Porto Timoni Beach offers a true escape from the bustling tourist hotspots.

4. Agni Bay Beach:
Nestled along Corfu's northeastern coast lies Agni Bay Beach, a discreet haven that captivates the senses. Known for its calm turquoise waters and pebbled shoreline, this secluded beach presents an ideal spot for private sunbathing and unwinding. Book a traditional taverna nearby and savor fresh seafood delicacies while sipping on a glass of locally-produced wine.

5. Issos Beach:
Located on the southern end of the island, Issos Beach is a hidden paradise boasting breathtaking landscapes and vast sandy dunes. With its unspoiled natural beauty, this secluded spot offers a peaceful escape from the crowded tourist hotspots. Take leisurely walks along the shoreline, let the sand tickle your toes, and become captivated by the untouched charm of Issos Beach.

6. Almyros Beach:
Tucked away on the northeast coast of Corfu, Almyros Beach offers serene seclusion and raw beauty. Known for its calm and shallow waters, this hidden gem is perfect for families with children who want to enjoy a safe swim. As you relax on the soft sand, allow the gentle sea breeze to carry your worries away, leaving you feeling refreshed and at peace.

Beach Activities and Water Sports

Corfu's beaches not only provide picturesque landscapes but also endless opportunities for exciting adventures and water sports. Whether you're a thrill-seeker or a laid-back vacationer, indulge in the following beach activities and water sports:

1. Scuba Diving:
Explore the magical underwater world of Corfu by embarking on a scuba diving

adventure. Encounter colorful marine life, marvel at beautiful coral reefs, and uncover hidden treasures beneath the surface. Dive centers located around the island offer courses suitable for beginners and experienced divers alike.

2. Parasailing:
Get a bird's-eye view of Corfu's stunning coastline as you soar high above the azure waters through parasailing. Experience the rush of adrenaline and witness the island's remarkable beauty from a unique perspective. No prior experience is necessary, as trained professionals will ensure your safety and guide you through the exhilarating experience.

3. Jet Skiing:
For those seeking an exhilarating water sport, jet skiing is the ultimate adventure. Feel the rush of adrenaline as you zip across the waves, taking in the stunning coastline of Corfu. Enjoy the feeling of the

wind in your hair and the thrill of speed as you zip across the waves on a jet ski. Rent a jet ski and venture out on your own or join a guided tour, allowing you to explore hidden corners of the coast while feeling the invigorating spray of seawater on your face.

4. Snorkeling:
Embrace the magic of snorkeling as you discover an underwater paradise thriving beneath the azure Mediterranean waters. Admire the colorful fish, explore hidden coves, and marvel at the mesmerizing coral reefs. With masks, fins, and snorkels readily available, snorkeling is a popular activity accessible to all age groups.

Iconic Coastlines and Cliffside Views

Corfu is blessed with dramatic coastlines that showcase nature's raw beauty. Corfu is renowned for its iconic coastlines, where towering cliffs meet the sparkling sea, creating breathtaking vistas. These dramatic landscapes offer unforgettable panoramic views that are a photographer's dream.

1. Cape Drastis:

Located on the northwestern tip of Corfu, Cape Drastis provides awe-inspiring views of towering limestone cliffs plunging into the sea. Witness the dramatic interplay of pristine azure waters, hidden caves, and rocky outcrops. You can either enjoy these vistas from the top or take a boat tour around the cape, allowing you to explore its hidden caves and admire the rugged beauty up close.

2. Paleokastritsa Cliffside Views:

Journey to Paleokastritsa to experience the mesmerizing cliffside views the island has to offer. From vantage points high above the sea, gaze upon a patchwork of turquoise waters, vibrant greenery, and distant islands. The scenic beauty of Paleokastritsa will leave you captivated and is best enjoyed during golden hour when the sun's warm hues cast a magical glow over the landscape.

3. Sidari Canal d'Amour:
Sidari's Canal d'Amour, meaning "Channel of Love," is a geological marvel that leaves visitors in awe. Formed by natural erosions over thousands of years, its narrow canals and secluded coves create a romantic, enchanting atmosphere. Legend has it that couples who swim through the canal will find eternal love, making it a must-visit spot for lovers and explorers alike.

4. Loggas Beach:
Situated on the scenic northwest coast of Corfu, Loggas Beach offers a stunning showcase of nature's artistry. The beach is famous for its towering cliffs that provide mesmerizing panoramic views of the Ionian Sea. As the sun dips below the horizon, the sky sets ablaze with vivid hues, creating a

spectacle that will forever be etched in your memory.

5. Peroulades Beach:
Located near Sidari, Peroulades Beach provides another opportunity to witness Corfu's extraordinary coastline. This viewpoint offers breathtaking vistas of the rugged cliffs and azure sea below. Grab a seat at the cliffside tavernas and indulge in local delicacies as you savor the sights and sounds of the Mediterranean.

As you embark on your journey to explore Corfu's magnificent beaches, hidden gems, engaging beach activities, and iconic coastlines, immersing yourself in the beauty and charm of this Greek paradise will undoubtedly create memories that will last a lifetime. May your adventures in Corfu be filled with sunshine, relaxation, and an indelible love for this enchanting island.

In conclusion, Corfu's top beaches, hidden gems, thrilling water sports, and iconic coastlines offer a diverse range of experiences. Whether you seek relaxation, adventure, or a chance to appreciate nature's wonders, this Greek paradise has something for everyone. So, pack your bags, book your tickets, and let Corfu beckon you with its sunkissed beaches, majestic coastlines, and memories waiting to be made.

CHAPTER FIVE

CUISINE AND DINING

1. Traditional Corfiot Food:

Corfu, the breathtaking Greek island nestled in the Ionian Sea, is not only famous for its pristine beaches and stunning coastlines but also for its mouthwatering traditional cuisine. The vibrant flavors and enticing aromas of Corfiot food will take you on a cultural journey that will linger in your memories long after you've left this paradise.

Renowned for its rich history and diverse influences, Corfu's culinary scene offers a delightful blend of Mediterranean, Italian, and French flavors. Traditional Corfiot dishes are characterized by the abundant use of local, fresh ingredients, aromatic herbs, and native olive oil, creating a symphony of tastes that will captivate your senses.

One must-try dish that represents the essence of Corfu's gastronomy is the Sofrito. This savory delight consists of thin slices of tender veal slowly simmered in a luscious sauce made from garlic, white wine, and vinegar. The meat is cooked to perfection, resulting in a melt-in-your-mouth experience that will leave you craving more.

Another staple of Corfiot cuisine is Bourdeto, a spicy fish stew bursting with flavors. This local specialty pairs fresh fish, typically scorpion fish or cod, with vibrant red chilies, garlic, tomatoes, and a splash of local wine. The combination of ingredients creates a symphony of flavors that will enchant your taste buds.

Vegetarians and vegans will be delighted by the variety of options available in Corfu.

Gemista, a classic Greek dish, features bell peppers or tomatoes stuffed with a flavorful mixture of rice, aromatic herbs, and fragrant local spices. This hearty meal is a testament to the island's commitment to using fresh, seasonal produce.

For those with a sweet tooth, Corfu offers an array of delectable desserts. The popular and refreshing Kumquat Spoon Sweets are a true delicacy. Made from the island's famous kumquats, these sweet preserves are served over a spoon and savored slowly, allowing their citrusy flavors to dance on your palate.

2. Popular Restaurants and Local Eateries:

Corfu's culinary landscape is dotted with an array of charming restaurants and bustling local eateries that will satisfy even the most discerning food enthusiasts. From cozy family-run tavernas to upscale dining establishments, there is something for every palate and preference.

If you're seeking an authentic Corfiot dining experience, head to Klimataria, a cozy taverna tucked away in the streets of Corfu Town. Serving traditional dishes with a contemporary twist, Klimataria enchants diners with its warm ambience and impeccable service. Don't miss their signature dish, the Souvlaki Me Pita, succulent grilled meat wrapped in a fluffy, homemade pita bread.

For a more refined culinary affair, visit Restaurant Etrusco, situated in the heart of Corfu Town. This elegant eatery offers a fusion of Italian and Greek cuisine, showcasing the island's best flavors in a fine-dining setting. Indulge in their signature dish, Ravioli al Pomodoro, delicate handcrafted pasta enveloping a tantalizing tomato filling.

If you find yourself in the picturesque village of Lakones, a visit to The Bellavista Taverna is a must. Perched atop a hill, this charming establishment boasts breathtaking views of Paleokastritsa Bay while delighting diners with an extensive menu of Corfiot specialties. Be sure to sample their velvety Moussaka, a comforting dish made from layers of potatoes, eggplant, and seasoned minced meat, topped with a creamy béchamel sauce.

3. Culinary Delights and Must-Try Dishes:

When exploring Corfu, it is impossible to resist the abundance of culinary delights that await. From traditional village dishes to seafood feasts, Corfu's gastronomic offerings will leave an indelible mark on your taste buds. Here are a few must-try dishes to experience the true flavors of the island.

Start your culinary adventure with a mouthful of Pastitsada. This hearty dish combines succulent chunks of slow-cooked beef or chicken with pasta, onions, garlic, and a medley of aromatic spices. The result is a symphony of flavors that will transport you to the heart of Corfiot heritage.

Seafood lovers will rejoice in the delicate flavors of Bourdetto, a spicy fish stew that tantalizes the taste buds with its combination of fresh fish, tomatoes, onions, and fiery chili peppers. Served with crusty bread, this dish showcases the island's bountiful seafood and will leave you longing for more seaside feasts.

For a lighter yet equally satisfying option, indulge in a plate of Pantzaria, a salad composed of rich, earthy beets, complemented by creamy feta cheese, walnuts, and a drizzle of local olive oil. This colorful and refreshing salad provides an explosion of flavors and textures that will rejuvenate even the weariest traveler.

End your culinary journey on a sweet note with a traditional Corfiot dessert, Rovani. This velvety semolina cake is drenched in a fragrant mixture of cinnamon, sugar, and syrup, creating a delightful treat to satisfy your sweet tooth.

4. Wine Tasting and Gastronomic Experiences:

Corfu's gastronomic offerings extend beyond its delicious cuisine. The island is also a haven for wine enthusiasts, boasting a rich history of winemaking and a diverse range of local vineyards and wineries to explore.

To truly appreciate the island's viticulture, embark on a wine tasting journey. Visit Theotoky Estate, a family-owned winery deeply rooted in tradition, and savor the fruity notes of their elegant white wines made from grape varieties such as Robola and Malagousia. Take a stroll through their vineyards, bask in the Mediterranean sun, and delight in the idyllic scenery while sipping on a glass of their award-winning wine.

For an immersive gastronomic experience, consider booking a vineyard tour and culinary workshop at Domaine Skouras, where you can learn about organic farming practices and the art of winemaking while relishing the flavors of their exquisite red wines. Guided by passionate experts, you'll have the opportunity to create your own delicious wine-infused recipes and savor them amidst the picturesque vineyards.

Corfu's culinary and oenological delights are best experienced first-hand, and these wine tasting and gastronomic experiences will leave you with a deeper understanding and appreciation of the island's rich traditions and flavors.

In conclusion, a sojourn to Corfu wouldn't be complete without indulging in its traditional cuisine, exploring popular restaurants and local eateries, relishing its culinary delights, and partaking in the island's wine tasting and gastronomic experiences. From the tantalizing flavors of Sofrito and Bourdeto to the soulful sweetness of Rovani and the rich heritage of Corfiot winemaking, each bite and sip reflect the warmth and richness of this Greek paradise. Prepare to embark on an extraordinary culinary journey that will satiate your senses and leave you yearning for more.

CHAPTER SIX

CULTURE AND FESTIVALS

1. Rich Cultural Heritage of Corfu:
Corfu, the jewel of the Ionian Sea, boasts a rich cultural heritage that entices travelers from all corners of the globe. Steeped in history, this Greek island offers a captivating blend of Venetian, French, and British influences that have shaped its unique identity.

At the heart of Corfu's cultural tapestry lies its magnificent Old Town, a UNESCO World Heritage Site that transports visitors back in time. Here, wander through narrow cobblestone streets lined with pastel-hued buildings, and stumble upon architectural wonders such as the Venetian Fortress, a testament to the island's medieval past.

Corfu's cultural legacy is further enhanced by the sheer number of palaces, mansions, and churches that dot its landscape. One cannot miss the Achilleion Palace, a captivating structure commissioned by Empress Elisabeth of Austria, adorned with classical Greek statues and breathtaking views of the sea. Another prominent landmark is the iconic Liston, an elegant architectural marvel reminiscent of Paris' Rue de Rivoli, offering a delightful setting for leisurely strolls and alfresco dining.

2. Traditional Festivals and Events:
Corfu's calendar is replete with vibrant traditional festivals and events that celebrate its rich heritage. The island comes alive each year with the joyous fervor of these cultural extravaganzas, drawing locals and visitors alike into a whirlwind of music, dance, and culinary delights.

One event that beautifully highlights Corfu's cultural identity is the Corfu Carnival. Spanning several weeks leading up to Lent, this exuberant festival showcases impressive processions of floats, dazzling costumes, and lively music. Witnessing the radiance and vibrancy of the carnival is an experience that will forever be etched in your memory.

Throughout the year, Corfu also celebrates numerous religious festivals, paying homage to its deeply rooted Orthodox Christian traditions. The most notable of these is Easter, when the island comes alive with candlelit processions, melodious hymns, and feasts of traditional Greek delicacies.

3. Museums and Art Galleries:
For art enthusiasts and history buffs, Corfu offers an exquisite range of museums and art galleries that shed light on its past and present artistic endeavors.

The Archaeological Museum is a treasure trove of ancient artifacts, showcasing the island's rich historical heritage. From intricate pottery to marble sculptures, marvel at the artistic prowess of civilizations that once thrived on these shores.

Art lovers will find solace within the walls of the Museum of Asian Art, boasting an impressive collection of Chinese, Japanese, and Indian art. The museum's serene ambiance creates the perfect backdrop for contemplation and appreciation.

Corfu's vibrant art scene also extends beyond museums, with a plethora of galleries that showcase the works of local and international artists. Explore these intimate spaces, where the brushstrokes of talented individuals perfectly capture the essence of the island's natural beauty and cultural diversity.

4. Local Crafts and Souvenirs:
When it comes to unique keepsakes and authentic craftsmanship, Corfu presents a delightful array of local crafts and souvenirs that make for cherished mementos of your visit.

Embark on a journey through the island's markets and boutiques, where you'll discover skilled artisans painstakingly creating Corfu's renowned silver jewelry and intricate embroideries. These traditional crafts embody the spirit of Corfu, their timeless beauty a reflection of the island's heritage.

As you wander the streets, your senses will be tantalized by the scent of spices permeating the air. The distinct flavors of local delicacies such as the Corfu Koum Kouat liqueur, olive oil products, and local sweets like mandolato and pasteli are enticing additions to any traveler's kitchen.

To truly immerse yourself in Corfu's culture, consider taking home a piece of local pottery or a woven reed basket, both traditional crafts preserved over centuries and effortlessly blending functionality and beauty.

Let Corfu's rich cultural heritage, traditional festivals, museums, art galleries, and local crafts beckon you toward an enchanting exploration of this Greek paradise. With its sunkissed beaches and majestic coastlines, this captivating island awaits to offer you an experience like no other.

CHAPTER SEVEN

DAY TRIPS AND EXCURSIONS

Exploring Corfu's Surrounding Islands

Corfu, known as the Emerald of the Ionian Sea, is not only a captivating destination in its own right but also serves as the perfect starting point to explore the surrounding islands that dot the azure waters of Greece.

From the charming village of Paleokastritsa to the breathtaking beaches of Paxi and Antipaxi, each island has a unique allure that beckons adventurers from all corners of the world. Delve into the enchanting world of Corfu's surrounding islands and embark on an exhilarating journey where history, stunning landscapes, and vibrant culture intertwine.

Venture northwest from Corfu to reach Paxi, a hidden gem embraced by translucent waters and remarkable rock formations. Arriving on the island, you'll be greeted by charming villages like Gaios and Lakka, where colorful houses and traditional tavernas line picturesque harbors. Explore the hidden coves, sunbathe on secluded beaches, or take a boat trip to the mesmerizing Blue Caves, where the sunlight filters through the crystalline waters, creating a magical display of colors.

A short distance southwest of Paxi, discover the captivating island of Antipaxi, known for its mesmerizing beaches and vineyards. Immerse yourself in the lush green landscapes as you explore the island's hidden trails, marvel at the vibrant corals during a snorkeling expedition or indulge in the local produce with a glass of the unique Antipaxi wine.

Boat Tours and Cruises

Embark on an unforgettable adventure as you set sail on the crystal-clear waters surrounding Corfu. Boat tours and cruises provide an opportunity to explore hidden coves, secluded beaches, and captivating landscapes that are not accessible by road.

Cruise along the coastline of Corfu, its picturesque old town rising majestically in the distance, the scent of olive trees lingering in the salty sea air. Feel the gentle breeze on your face as you explore the mythical sea caves of Nafsika or anchor near the dazzling beaches of Barbati and Glyfada for a refreshing swim in the turquoise waters.

For a more immersive experience, board a sailing yacht and journey to the remote islands of Mathraki or Othoni. As the sails catch the wind, surrender to the tranquility of the open sea and let the rhythm of the waves guide your journey. Snorkel in hidden bays, hike along uncharted trails, or simply unwind on the deck as you gaze upon the stunning coastline and immerse yourself in the essence of Greek island life.

Hiking and Nature Walks

Corfu showcases a landscape brimming with natural beauty, offering hiking and nature enthusiasts an array of trails to discover. Lace up your hiking boots and prepare to be captivated by Corfu's breathtaking vistas and diverse ecosystems.

Begin your journey at the lush Corfu Trail, a long-distance footpath that spans the entire length of the island, immersing you in its rich flora and fauna. Meander through olive groves, meadows adorned with wildflowers, and dense forests of cypress and pine. From panoramic viewpoints overlooking the emerald sea to secluded waterfalls hidden within the island's interior, each step unveils a new layer of Corfu's enchanting allure.

For a more condensed hiking experience, explore the scenic trails of Mount Pantokrator, Corfu's highest peak. Ascend through the gentle slopes, passing traditional villages, ancient monasteries, and terraced vineyards. As you reach the summit, be rewarded with a panoramic view that transcends beyond the island and into the sparkling Ionian Sea, painting an awe-inspiring canvas you'll never forget.

Historic Excursions

Corfu is a treasure trove of history, with a fascinating past that has shaped its architecture, culture, and traditions. Embark on historic excursions that offer insight into the island's rich heritage and remarkable landmarks.

Start your journey in Corfu Town, a UNESCO World Heritage site, and stroll through the narrow alleys of the Venetian-inspired Old Town. Admire the imposing fortresses of the New and Old Fortress, witness the grandeur of the Liston promenade, and explore the elegant Spianada Square. Delve into the island's Byzantine and Venetian past at the Museum of Asian Art, the Corfu Archaeological Museum, or the Byzantine Museum.

Beyond the city walls, venture inland to visit the Achilleion Palace, a grand neoclassical mansion built by Empress Elisabeth of Austria, also known as Sisi. Wander through its opulent rooms, adorned with exquisite artwork and surrounded by meticulously manicured gardens. Stand in awe of the iconic statue of Achilles, a symbol of heroism and a testament to love and beauty.

Corfu is a crossroads of cultures and civilizations, and a visit to its charming villages unveils a tapestry of stories waiting to be discovered. Explore the traditional mountain village of Old Perithia, the island's oldest inhabited village. As you wander through its stone-paved streets and immaculately preserved houses, you'll be transported to a bygone era, immersing yourself in the island's rural charm.

With these extensive details about exploring Corfu's surrounding islands, boat tours and cruises, hiking and nature walks, and historic excursions, my dear readers will be fully equipped to embark on an extraordinary journey through the wonders of this Greek paradise.

CHAPTER EIGHT

PRACTICAL TIPS AND USEFUL INFORMATION

Local Customs and Etiquette

Corfu, a Greek paradise beckoning you with sun-kissed beaches and majestic coastlines, is not only renowned for its natural beauty but also for its rich cultural heritage. When visiting this enchanting island, it is important to familiarize yourself with the local customs and etiquette to ensure a truly immersive experience. By understanding and respecting the traditions of Corfu, you will forge a deeper connection with its vibrant spirit.

Hospitality is at the heart of Corfiot culture. As soon as you set foot on this island, you will be overwhelmed by the warm and welcoming nature of the locals. It is customary to greet people with a smile and a friendly "kalimera" (good morning) during the day, or "kalispera" (good evening) later in the day. The Corfiots take pride in their hospitality and embrace visitors as if they were long-lost friends.

When dining in Corfu, it is customary to wait for your host or hostess to invite you to sit down. Keep in mind that Greeks take their meals slowly and consider eating a social activity. It is common for a meal to last several hours, with multiple courses being served. Engage in lively conversation and savor each dish, as you become part of this convivial experience.

Covering up when visiting churches or monasteries is crucial to show respect. Both men and women should wear modest clothing that covers their shoulders and knees. Additionally, it is considered impolite to enter and walk through a church during a religious service, so plan your visits accordingly.

Greek people are generally affectionate and expressive, known for their warm gestures. Don't be surprised if locals greet you with a hug or a kiss on each cheek if they are close acquaintances. However, it is essential to be sensitive to personal boundaries and gauge the level of familiarity before engaging in such gestures.

Safety Guidelines and Health Information

Ensuring your safety and well-being is paramount when exploring Corfu. By adhering to some essential safety guidelines and being aware of health information, you can focus on enjoying the beauty of this Greek paradise with peace of mind.

Corfu is a very safe destination for travelers, but as with any place, it is important to exercise caution. Keep an eye on your belongings, especially in crowded areas and tourist hotspots. Furthermore, be cautious when interacting with strangers and avoid sharing personal information unless necessary.

In terms of health information, it is recommended to have comprehensive travel insurance that covers medical expenses. Carry a first aid kit for minor injuries or ailments, and make sure to comply with any necessary vaccinations or precautions advised by your healthcare provider before traveling. Always carry and drink bottled water to stay hydrated, especially during the warm summer months.

Transportation and Getting Around

Transportation in Corfu offers a variety of options, ensuring easy accessibility for visitors to explore all the island has to offer. Whether you prefer the convenience of driving or the charm of public transportation, getting around Corfu is a breeze.

Renting a car is a popular choice for independent exploration. Several car rental agencies are available both at the airport and in major towns. Having your own vehicle grants you the freedom to venture off the beaten path, discovering hidden beaches and picturesque mountain villages that are not easily accessible by public transport.

Alternatively, Corfu boasts a reliable public transportation network. Local buses connect the main towns and top tourist destinations, with regular routes and affordable fares. The central bus terminal is located in Corfu Town, from where you can plan your itineraries and comfortably reach various parts of the island.

Taxis are also abundant in Corfu and provide a convenient means of transportation. Look for licensed taxis with meters, and make sure the driver activates it at the beginning of your journey. It is advisable to agree on a fare beforehand for longer trips or negotiate if meters are unavailable.

Shopping and Souvenirs

No travel experience is complete without indulging in a bit of shopping and bringing home unique souvenirs to cherish the memories of your trip. Corfu offers a delightful range of shopping options, blending traditional crafts with modern boutiques.

When it comes to traditional crafts, seek out local artisanal shops to find handcrafted goods that exemplify the island's heritage. From delicate silver jewelry to intricate ceramics and intricate lacework, you will discover treasures that reflect the rich cultural traditions of Corfu.

For a modern shopping experience, visit the vibrant streets of Corfu Town, lined with trendy boutiques and high-end fashion stores. Stroll through the bustling Esplanade or explore the narrow alleys of Liston, where you can find an eclectic mix of designer brands and artisanal products.

For those looking for authentic local products, delight your taste buds with olive oil, honey, and regional delicacies. Remember to check the packaging for certifications that ensure the authenticity and quality of the products you wish to purchase.

In conclusion, Corfu not only mesmerizes with its natural beauty but also immerses visitors in a cultural experience like no other. By embracing the local customs, acting responsibly, and being prepared for your journey, you can ensure a memorable and enriching trip while exploring this Greek paradise. Happy travels!

CHAPTER NINE

FAMILY FUN ON THE ISLAND: DISCOVERING CORFU WITH CHILDREN

Welcome to Corfu, a breathtaking Greek island that offers an unforgettable experience for families seeking fun and adventure. With its picturesque landscapes, crystal-clear turquoise waters, and warm hospitality, Corfu has something to offer for everyone, including the little ones. Join us as we embark on this journey of discovery, tailored to create precious memories with your children.

1. Perfect Beaches for Family Fun:
Corfu boasts an array of stunning beaches, providing the perfect backdrop for endless

hours of family enjoyment. Whether your children love building sandcastles on the soft golden shores or exploring the rock pools teeming with marine life, Corfu has it all. Don't miss the child-friendly Glyfada Beach, which offers shallow waters and a relaxed atmosphere ideal for family picnics. Another popular choice is Benitses Beach, known for its vibrant seafront and exciting water sports activities.

2. Exploring Ancient History:
Corfu is steeped in rich history, and what better way to inspire young minds than by delving into the island's fascinating past? Visit the Achilleion Palace, once a residence for the Empress of Austria, and let your children imagine themselves as kings and queens. Explore the remains of the Old Fortress, where knights once strolled, or take a trip to the Mon Repos Estate, surrounded by lush greenery and ancient ruins, where mythology comes alive.

3. Adventure in Nature:
Corfu's natural beauty provides the perfect playground for adventure-loving families. Take a hike through the stunning Corfu Trail, with its breathtaking vistas at every turn. Your children will be captivated by the diverse flora and fauna along the way. For a unique experience, head to the Aqualand Water Park, filled with thrilling water slides, lazy rivers, and exciting splash pads for all ages. Get ready for a day of splashing fun and shrieks of delight.

4. Cruising the Sea:
Corfu's turquoise waters beckon families to embark on an unforgettable adventure aboard a boat tour. Explore hidden coves, discover secret sea caves, and snorkel in vibrant underwater worlds. Sailing around the island on a private yacht or joining a group excursion, families can bond over the beauty of the Ionian Sea and create incredible memories that will last a lifetime.

As you plan your Corfu adventure, remember that the island is a treasure trove of family-friendly activities, wellness sanctuaries, and countless opportunities to reconnect with nature and yourself. Let Corfu be the stage where you create memories to cherish forever—a paradise that welcomes all backgrounds, races, and genders with open arms.

CHAPTER TEN

WELLNESS RETREATS IN PARADISE: REJUVENATION AND RELAXATION IN CORFU

Escape to the paradise of Corfu, a haven of tranquility and natural beauty that offers a myriad of wellness retreats. Surrender to the soothing embrace of the island as you rejuvenate your body, mind, and spirit. Indulge in the healing power of nature and embark on a journey of self-discovery.

1. Serenity in Nature:

Corfu's unspoiled landscapes create the perfect backdrop for a blissful wellness retreat. Immerse yourself in the island's lush olive groves, walk along scenic trails, and breathe in the crisp, invigorating air. The peaceful surroundings will help you achieve tranquility and connect with the essence of Corfu's natural beauty.

2. Yoga and Meditation:
Corfu offers an array of tranquil spaces that invite visitors to practice yoga and meditation. Join a class taught by experienced instructors or indulge in a private session amidst nature's embrace. Let the gentle sea breeze and the sounds of waves crashing against the shore guide you into a state of deep relaxation and self-awareness.

3. Revitalizing Spa Experiences:
Pamper yourself with rejuvenating spa treatments using locally-sourced ingredients, such as olive oil, lavender, and citrus. From hot stone massages to therapeutic aromatherapy sessions, Corfu's spas offer a holistic approach to wellness. Indulge in a luxurious massage overlooking the sea, taking in the panoramic views that

will leave you feeling revitalized and renewed.

4. Mindful Cuisine:

Corfu is renowned for its fresh and healthy Mediterranean cuisine, known to nourish both body and soul. Sample the island's delectable dishes made with local produce, infused with flavors that will delight your taste buds. From traditional Greek delicacies to international vegan options, Corfu's culinary offerings will leave you feeling nourished, energized, and satisfied.

CHAPTER ELEVEN

CONCLUSION

Lasting Impressions of Corfu

Welcome to Corfu, the enchanting island nestled in the turquoise waters of the Ionian Sea. From the moment you step foot on this Greek paradise, you will be greeted with breathtaking landscapes, rich history, and warm hospitality. Prepare to be captivated by the mesmerizing blend of ancient charm and natural splendor that Corfu has to offer.

As you embark on your journey to discover Corfu, one of the reasons why this island leaves a lasting impression on its visitors is the unparalleled beauty of its beaches. The sun-kissed shores, framed by majestic coastlines, offer a tranquil escape, inviting you to unwind and soak up the

Mediterranean sun. Whether you prefer secluded coves or vibrant beachfronts buzzing with activity, Corfu caters to all tastes.

One such beach that is guaranteed to take your breath away is Paleokastritsa. With its crystal-clear waters, nestled between verdant cliffs, this slice of paradise seems almost too perfect to be real. As you dive into the refreshing sea, you'll be mesmerized by the vibrant marine life, making it an ideal spot for snorkeling enthusiasts.

If you're longing for a more secluded getaway, head to Myrtiotissa beach. Tucked away on the island's western coast, Myrtiotissa offers a paradise-like retreat, accessible only through a short scenic hike. Once you reach the beach, you'll be rewarded with soft golden sand and azure waters, providing an idyllic setting to escape the hustle and bustle of everyday life.

In addition to its stunning beaches, Corfu's charm lies in its rich history. As you explore its ancient ruins and fortresses, you'll find yourself stepping back in time. The Old Town of Corfu, a UNESCO World Heritage site, is a maze of narrow streets, lined with traditional Venetian buildings. Take a leisurely stroll through its atmospheric alleys, visit the imposing Liston, and lose yourself in the vibrant ambiance of the Spianada, the largest square in the Balkans.

If you're a history aficionado, a visit to the Achilleion Palace is a must. Built as a tribute to the mythical hero Achilles, this neoclassical palace offers a fascinating insight into the opulent lifestyle of Empress Elisabeth of Austria. From the well-preserved gardens to the ornate interiors adorned with stunning frescoes, the Achilleion Palace is a testament to Corfu's historical significance.

But Corfu is not just about its natural beauty and historical landmarks. The island is also a gastronomic paradise for food enthusiasts. Indulge in an array of traditional Greek dishes, from fresh seafood caught daily to mouthwatering local delicacies such as Pastitsada and Sofrito. With its thriving culinary scene, Corfu tantalizes your taste buds with a diverse fusion of flavors that will leave you craving more.

Your next adventure awaits!

Are you ready to embark on a new adventure and explore the wonders of Corfu? Delve into the unique landscapes, immerse yourself in the island's rich heritage, and enjoy the warm embrace of Greek hospitality. Whether you're a nature lover, history enthusiast, or simply seeking solace on sun-drenched shores, Corfu promises to leave an indelible mark on your heart.

As you plan your journey through Corfu, prepare to be greeted by breathtaking beaches that beckon you to embrace the sea. Sink your toes into soft golden sands, take a dip in clear turquoise waters, and allow the gentle rhythm of the waves to wash away your worries. Corfu's beaches are a gateway to tranquility and relaxation, offering a sense of calm rarely found elsewhere.

Beyond its pristine beaches, Corfu is a living testament to its fascinating history. Explore ancient ruins that whisper tales of civilizations past, wander through narrow cobblestone streets that bear witness to centuries of tradition, and traverse mighty fortresses that stood against the test of time. Corfu's rich heritage is a treasure trove waiting to be unraveled, captivating history buffs and curious travelers alike.

No adventure in Corfu would be complete without indulging in its vibrant culinary scene. Delight your taste buds with authentic Greek flavors, from tangy feta cheese and juicy olives to succulent grilled meats and aromatic herbs. Embark on a gastronomic journey that will awaken your senses and leave you yearning for more, all amidst picturesque landscapes and charming seaside tavernas.

Corfu's allure lies not only in its sights but also in the genuine warmth of its people. Experience the famed Greek hospitality firsthand, as locals welcome you with genuine smiles and open hearts. Whether it's a heartfelt conversation with a friendly shopkeeper or an impromptu dance at a lively traditional festival, Corfu invites you to become a part of its vibrant tapestry.

So, pack your bags, seize this opportunity, and let the allure of Corfu transport you to a world where nature's beauty intertwines with ancient tales, creating memories to last a lifetime. Unleash the wanderlust within, for your next adventure awaits in this Greek paradise that is Corfu.

Printed in Great Britain
by Amazon